CONTENTS

THE GREATEST TREASURE EVER SHARED

Chapter One

Isaiah 33:6
"He will be the sure foundation for your times, a rich store of salvation and wisdom and knowledge; the fear of the Lord is the key to this treasure."

Golden statues. Two-thousand year old mosaics. Egyptian mummies. Splinters claimed to be from the cross. A spear that's said to have pierced Jesus' side. Greek and Roman marble sculptures. Michelangelo masterpieces. Gold and silver threaded tapestries studded with pearls and jewels. Enough precious artwork that if it were lined up side by side, it would wrap around the entire Vatican City nearly 5 times. Over 58 miles of artifacts, precious books, artwork and treasures make up the Vatican Museums and Archives. It is said that if you spent a mere 60 seconds in front of each display in the museum, it would take you well over 6 consecutive years to see each piece. This doesn't include the 52 miles of archives that lay beneath the museum. Its value is beyond priceless, but scholars have estimated its worth to be around $15 billion - or maybe more.

As we wandered around the marble covered halls with golden mosaic ceilings, we marveled at the treasures stretched out before our very eyes. Our feet trudged across 2,000 year old mosaics in pristine condition, moved from their original homes to crown the floors of the Popes' with their splendor. Our eyes perused the precious works of art and were caught by the glinting jewels that danced in the sunlight. Our mouths hung open at the ancient manuscripts and the papyrus scrolls that hung on the walls.

As we entered one such room filled with so much splendor, our extremely expressive tour guide held her arms open wide and spun around in a circle as she detailed the expansiveness of the Pope's collection. She smiled broadly as she discussed the treasures that were hidden below our very feet and proudly asserted that "amongst the 58 miles of this treasure trove, there is enough treasure, that if used properly, it could change the entire world. It could rewrite history."

This phrase quickly caught my ear, arrested my heart and felt quite literally like a punch to my gut. Here we are, gathering enough treasure for ourselves that if we used it right, it could change the world. It could rewrite history. And yet, here it sits, most never even seen, sitting in a dark room in the furthest recesses, completely hidden beneath our feet.

The human side of me quickly became cynical and critical. Why would we gather such immense treasure for ourselves? Why, if we could change the world, are we instead charging admission and capitalizing upon our own wealth, our own fortune, our own perceived blessing?

It hit me as I stood admiring one of the greatest treasures known in existence, criticizing in my heart the collectors of such splendor for missing their chance to effectively change the world, that they are not the only ones who have hoarded the blessing for themselves. I, too, have missed the mark. You see, I've been given the greatest treasure in existence. It was a free gift offered to me. It's greater than Roman ruins or Greek artifacts. It's more beautiful than silver and gold stranded tapestries. It's more precious than jewels and paintings.

It's authentic. It's rugged. It's priceless. It's holy.

Christ died on my behalf. He paid my penalty. He covered me with his righteousness, and He offered me eternal life with him. There is no greater treasure than that.

But it doesn't end there. He is offering the same thing to you.

Instead of intently spreading this amazing treasure to those around me, recognizing Christ's opportunity to rewrite history through my obedience, I've often kept it to myself. It's quite possible a tour guide might spin around the chambers of my heart with a smile and say, "There's enough treasure here that if used properly, it could change the world. It could rewrite history." And yet...here it sits.

The treasure grows deeper by the year, but instead of sharing it, I sometimes stash it deep in the recesses of the archives of my heart, and keep it for myself. Could He spread this immense wealth all on His own? Of course he could! But the joy He has when His people begin to look like Him, begin to act like Him - I'm quite sure that He's happy and hopeful to give us the chance to reflect Him to the world.

There is enough treasure stored in the archives of your heart that it could change the entire world, my friend. The treasure that you hold is one that, if used correctly, it could rewrite history. You have an opportunity to hold it for yourself, or to use it properly and effectively change the course of the entire world.

Share the treasure! Spread the wealth! Quit hoarding it all for yourself and enthusiastically share Jesus with this broken world. You're sharing the greatest, most valuable treasure known in existence. And here's the best news of all: there's plenty to go around!

"I DON'T KNOW!!"

Chapter Two

Proverbs 3:5-6
"*Trust in the LORD with all your heart and lean not on your own understanding. In all of your ways acknowledge Him and He will direct your paths.*"

We'd been sitting at the airport for a while, waiting for our plane to depart. We were in a foreign country, didn't speak the language well, and our gate had already changed multiple times. We had been assured that, this time, we were in the right place, and so we just rested and waited. As our scheduled boarding time approached, however, we began to get uneasy and began investigating the reason for the delay. There weren't many of us there, but the small group that had gathered together realized quickly that, once again, our gate had been changed, we had somehow missed the announcement, and we had better make a run for it to have any chance of making our flight. Snatching up our bags, we raced off through the airport, scanned our tickets at the boarding gate and tore off onto the open air tarmac, running aimlessly at an aircraft that was supposedly waiting for us somewhere out there. My husband and I were honeymooning, so with stars in our eyes we laughingly held hands through the stress. But I'll never forget this couple running beside us. She had her hands full of bags, scarves and who knows what all trailing behind her all the way across that hot tarmac. They were middle aged and had seen a bit more of life than we had. Half way across as we ran towards one of three, unidentified planes, she stopped, frantically grabbed his arm and pleaded in panic, "Wait, where are we going?"

He turned around, still running, with the most confounded,

stressed out, boiling red face. He bellowed back with white knuckled fists and shoulders raised clear to his ears, "I DON'T KNOW!!" as if it were one, long drawn out exclamation. With this little outburst, he then turned around and just kept aimlessly running.

It's become a bit of a joke to us through the years. Any time one of us is feeling a bit like the red faced temper tantrum on the tarmac, the other will exaggeratingly exclaim in fake exasperation, "I DON'T KNOW!"

To combat as many "I DON'T KNOW" moments in our marriage as possible, my husband and I have a bit of an agreement. Travel is a bit stressful to him, but it is life-giving to me, so early on in our marriage, we decided that he would travel with me as long as I worked out all of the details. He would adventure, as long as I removed as many of the stressful situations as possible. So, in recent years, as our kids have gotten older and our adventures have grown more complicated, I have organized our adventures and tried to plan them to a "T," to remove as many potential "I DON'T KNOW" mishaps as possible.

It was on one such trip around the world that this little arrangement taught me a valuable lesson while wandering around a brand new city. I knew our ultimate destination, and even what time we needed to be there. But as much as I had pre-planned and organized myself, I didn't know exactly HOW to reach our goal. I wasn't exactly worried, for I knew that as long as I held the map in my hand, we'd get there before long…perhaps with a few wrong turns and detours. But if it were up to me at all, we'd get there just the same, eventually.

It was in this moment, after we'd made several wrong turns (I'm quite sure I looked like that frantic lady with bags and kids flailing behind her), that my husband gently took the reins and offered to help. He determined that he would be the one to get us where we needed to go. So I put my trusty maps away and softly chuckled as he confidently took the lead, without a map. I was quickly put in my place, however, as my chuckles turned to marveling, and really complete awe. He would merely glance at the destination briefly on my trusty map, and then proceed to confidently lead his four little followers straight to the destination, every single time. Just a glance at the map and then we'd round a corner and poof! We'd arrive.

It was after our second jaw-dropping, seamless arrival to some location or another that it occurred to me that, left to my own devices, even with all the planning and studying and training that I'd done, I was afraid to take a single step without holding the map in my hand the entire time. Had I tried, it was sure to bring disaster at some point along the way. But my husband - he had this knack for just knowing the way to the destination. When I put my frantic worry away and simply trusted him to do it, he led us perfectly every single time.

Too often in our Christian journey we hold too tightly to our planning and studying and preparing. Sometimes all that planning and organization just gets in the way. Other times, we refuse to take a single step before we plan it to perfection. Still others, we run along frantically, aimlessly, just hoping we will get it all right.

In our chaos, we often forget that the key to this Christian life is not a perfect plan, nor is it perfect study. The key is a relationship. Far too often, we forget to stay close to Him, we forget to set our worry aside, and we forget to simply let Him lead.

While we may snicker at first at the idea of following Him without knowing our perfectly ordered steps ahead of time, and we may even frantically scream, "Wait, where are we going?" the ability to trust Him to lead is all that He asks. When we stop insisting on ordering our steps and simply follow Him, the journey is perfection. You'll sit back, watch and marvel at the perfect steps set out before you, and when you round that corner and see your ultimate destination come into view, you'll realize that red-faced temper tantrum you felt like throwing was useless in the end. He asks you to follow Him, but more than that, he invites you to trust him, and not to worry. His way is perfect, faster, safer and easier than yours ever was, and you'll be glad you simply trusted Him and just followed all the way.

DIFFERENT BUT PERFECT

Chapter Three

Isaiah 64:8
"But now, O Lord, you are our Father; we are the clay, and you are our potter; we are all the work of your hand."

I took in the pieces of my broken, chipped and shattered frame, and with it my heart, full of hope...

Having moved 13 times in our 16 years of marriage, inevitably we've had most of our worldly possessions damaged at one point or another. There are not many "things" that mean a lot to me. Not many material possessions hold much sentimental value. But there is one object that has symbolized "home" over the years. As soon as it is hung on the walls of our bedroom, no matter where we are in the world, we are home. My grandmother painted it for us as a wedding gift, and it has adorned the walls of our bedroom since day one of our marriage. It is one of those things that symbolizes our life, and it is precious. Sadly, it had its turn with our most recent move, to be broken.

Because of the nation-wide pandemic lockdown, this mangled frame has been dejectedly sitting in a corner of my bedroom, awaiting the day that I could have it repaired. I saved all the little pieces of the damaged frame and after months of complete closure, I was finally able to take it to a little framing shop that had recently reopened in our little village.

As I entered, a sweet, elderly lady greeted me. I asked her if she spoke English and she did not, but as she looked sympathetically at the broken pieces I held, she gestured towards a man at the back. Amongst all of the soft words uttered from her wrinkled lips that sounded much like gibberish to my untrained ears, one word I recognized: he was the "master."

He, too, did not speak English, my translator app wouldn't work in the store, and I was dismayed to realize through our pantomime conversation that the frame was damaged beyond repair. I'd have to pick out something new. I would never again have my picture be the way I had always known it and loved it.

Through gestures and guesses, I tried to choose a new frame and began to grieve even more, the damage to my treasure. With a lot of words I couldn't comprehend, the great master took my precious frame. With four gentle, decisive movements, he broke the four sides of my frame at their seams before my very eyes, and wrapped them up in tape. He placed them in my hands, and then he spoke. I didn't understand a word he said, but he reached out kindly, gently took the broken remnants back, and set them aside. The frame that I loved was gone. He took my picture, placed it carefully to the side and said, "Avrio," a word I recognized which means, "tomorrow." And so, after questioning "tomorrow" several times, with zero control, and no ability to express exactly what it is that I'm wanting, I had to just leave my treasure in the hands of the master, hope that he understood, and just trust. I walked out of that shop with the hope of tomorrow, leaving my treasure behind (but without a name or phone number or any way to identify me), and had to trust the master to do his restorative work. He had my broken treasure. I had nothing.

Once outside I crumbled into a puddle of tears, and almost panic. Zero control. Zero control. Zero control.

Do you ever feel as though you are taking your crumbled treasure before the Master? Your hopes, your dreams, your very life? And as you stand there sputtering all of YOUR desires, trying to control how He fixes it, or which new frame he puts it in, you're stuck speaking two different languages. While you may recognize one word here and another there, you are left with zero control. You are broken. You are helpless. And you are at the mercy of the Master.

Oh, my friend, what a beautiful, humbling place to be. Take your battered treasure to the Lord and just TRUST Him. He is the master. And while it may not look exactly how you have planned it out, He brings beauty from the ashes, and His skillful hand brings wholeness from the broken, tattered and torn. What you receive back, in the hope of tomorrow, when done through the Master's hands, is perfect.

I received my picture back the next day, as promised. And it was perfect. Different, but perfect. And in addition to the beautiful picture that was ready to finally be hung on my wall, I received the pieces of my old frame, prepared to be made into a smaller frame, if I will just trust him with another picture at a later date.

The hope of tomorrow is painful, but the work of the Master's hand is perfect.

TIP TOES AND T-REXES

Chapter Four

Psalm 100:2
"Worship the Lord with gladness; come before him with joyful songs."

Years ago, our middle son, Mason, was a dinosaur fanatic. He knew all the facts, all the species, all the details. He spent hours learning about them and reciting his knowledge to anyone who would listen. One day he saw an advertisement for a silver T-Rex skeleton necklace, and he decided I just HAD to have it. The sweet little guy brought me the computer, told me that he'd found this necklace and wanted to get it for me for Christmas. He had found something that he loved, and it made him think of me. He had no money, he had nothing to offer, but could he please get me a present?

What could a mother do but help her little boy procure such a thoughtful, heart-felt gift?

Upon its arrival, I helped my little one wrap it up, and he hid it from sight. Wouldn't you know, on Christmas morning, there was a little present tucked under the Christmas tree with "M-O-M" scrawled across it in giant letters.

My little blond-headed boy with the sparkly blue eyes and lopsided dimple in his cheek stood in front of me, joyfully wringing his hands together while I opened it, and he could hardly contain his excitement. Tip toes bounced up and down excitedly and little squeals of delight escaped his mouth in anticipation. When I opened the box, I gasped and ooh-ed and ahhh-ed over this little faux-silver dinosaur skeleton necklace, and his giggles of delight was the most precious gift I received that year.

Years later, I whisked Mason away for a few moments, just him and I. During these one on one times, he comes alive. He usually leads the conversation and that day was no exception. Out of the blue, he brought up the necklace he had given me years before. "Mom, I've always wondered, were you really surprised when I gave you that necklace? I always thought it was weird that you bought it. You paid for it. And then you were so delighted and surprised when I gave it to you."

With my heart warmed at the memory, I smiled and said, "No, I wasn't surprised. But you were so excited, and I took delight in you. I wanted you to have the joy of giving a gift."

Truly, to this day you'd be hard pressed to find a piece of jewelry that means more to me than my T-Rex necklace.

The conversation changed to deeper things and we began discussing worship. Struggles with not wanting to sing or pray aloud because of feeling self conscious and embarrassed are real, and frustrating. I had shared that not only does God want our worship, but he TELLS us to worship.

Why would the God of the universe desire our worship and praise?

Remember that dinosaur necklace Mason bought me? I paid for it. I already knew all about it. I didn't need it. But I delighted in it because it was from his heart. It's the same with God. He already paid for it. It's no secret…He knows all about it. He doesn't need it (ohh, but do you think it blesses Him? You better believe it!).

He may not need it, but you do! The gift you receive from joyfully, expectantly, excitedly offering to God what is already His, is beautiful. He wants to give you the joy of being able to offer a gift. He wants you to experience the mystery of His delight in you. And the joy that He has in watching you offer something to Him, well, there's nothing more beautiful to a parent, and God is no exception.

So this week, today, even, stand before your Father like my little blond haired boy with bouncing tip toes and contagious giggles offering a T-Rex necklace. Delight in Him, and He in you. Oh, the joy you will bring Him will warm his heart, and yours, for years to come.

CALL UPON ME

Chapter Five

Psalm 50:15
"Call upon Me in the day of trouble; I will deliver you, and you will honor Me."

I had always dreamed of being a missionary, and in Africa, no less, so my heart rejoiced at the opportunity to take a few weeks and join my husband in the land that held a very soft place in my heart. Chris had the opportunity to do a Medical Mission Rotation as part of his medical training in 2010. We worked side by side for the month that we were there and I reveled at being able to watch my husband do the work that the Lord had called him to do.

As our time in Kenya wound down, we had settled in the little village of Mukeu, far from the city of Nairobi. Life there was very different from the life we had seen in the city. It was quieter, and we found ourselves awakened in the wee hours of the morning not from cars and street noise and music, but from the rooster that had obnoxiously settled outside of our window. I can still smell the smoke that hung in the air from the outdoor kitchens. I can still hear the hollow whack of the rods on the backs of the donkeys as they carried heavy supplies down the roads. I can still feel the sticky rubber boots as we slipped them on our feet every morning to trudge through the thick mud for more than a mile to the village for the days' work.

One morning, as Chris worked tirelessly in the makeshift clinic and I filled prescriptions in the pharmacy, there was a commotion.

I watched as my husband went quickly flying out of the clinic, as fast as his little legs would carry him. I had no idea what was happening, and was a bit relieved when I learned that a lady had been working in the fields and she had fainted. They were just on their way to help her. After some time, here came that little entourage, covered in mud, huffing and puffing after carrying her through the thick muddy roads, bearing the weight of the sweet little lady amongst them. My relief from moments before dissipated quickly. Her intermittent unconscious state was only interrupted by brief periods of violent vomiting. She had had a stroke and was suffering from seizures.

We were in a little makeshift hut. There were none of the typical life saving measures available to us, yet they cleared a room and began doing everything they could. I stood, frozen in the "pharmacy."

My heart was racing and I feared the worst for this woman. As I listened to my husband's voice doing everything he could for this dear woman in the neighboring room, all I could do was stand there. Completely frozen.

My heart cried out to the Lord, with no words of my own. Upon the wall directly across from me was hung a tattered, dusty, yellowed paper from years before. Despite it being ragged and worn, it was as though it were suddenly written in bold and highlighted in the brightest neon yellow you could imagine, as it practically leapt off of the wall in front of me. Upon this tattered scrap was written:

> *"Call upon Me in the day of trouble; I will deliver you, and you will honor Me."* Psalm 50:15

In my immobile state, all I could do was read these words over and over and over again.

"Call upon me." For the woman.

"Call upon me." For my husband.
"Call upon me." For myself.

I read them and I prayed them and I claimed them. *"Call upon Me in the day of trouble; I will deliver you, and you will honor Me."* I knew God would deliver us, and we would honor Him.

And He did.

And we did.

For 11 years, I've thought often of this story. This very morning these words were brought to mind yet again. But this time, it occurred to me that so often, we - ahem, *I* - get the order wrong. Sometimes we think that it is because God delivered us (cause), that we then honor him (effect). But focusing on the deliverance is not what's important here. Me honoring Him is not contingent upon His deliverance. He receiving honor is contingent upon my trust.

It is not the fact that God delivers me that brings Him honor. It is the fact that I call upon Him. The idea that God will deliver me is a blessed one, and one that gives me great hope and great peace. But the thing that brings Him honor is the very fact that I ran to Him. I called on Him.
There is no greater honor we can bring to Him than to trust Him, even in our days of trouble. You see, whether God chooses to deliver me in the way I desire or even recognize is irrelevant. He is holy and worthy of glory and honor regardless. It is the act of recognizing my need for Him that honors Him, more than any recognition of His deliverance.

Call upon Him, my friends. You will honor Him.

THE YELLOW SHIRT

Chapter Six

Seventy-seven days. It doesn't seem like an especially long time, but when you're squeezing 5 people in a single-room hotel room, 77 days can feel like an eternity. After living in such a hotel room for months on end during a move halfway around the world, our little family had experienced a gambit of emotions. Cramming 5 family members into one room for such a length of time is sure to be fun and humbling and frustrating and, well, even sanctifying.

One day, while feeling particularly alone and different and frustrated as we adjusted to our new surroundings, our (then) precocious 8 year old, through a deluge of puddling, violent tears, collapsed into my arms and fairly shouted, "I feel like all of the world is wearing a red shirt. Everyone, except me. I'm wearing a yellow shirt, and as hard as I try, I have on this yellow shirt and I can't take it off. I just want to wear a red shirt like everyone else."

These words hit very close to this mother's heart of mine. So many things to unpack in that sentiment. So many deep, relatable emotions. So much wisdom and impressive imagery to come bubbling forth from a frame so very small. They have replayed over and over in my mind throughout the years, and I've often thought of this uncomfortable, hated, beautiful yellow shirt.

We are currently living in an overseas environment and we often play a game we've affectionately named, "Red Shirts." How long will it take before the clerk notices we are a foreigner and switches to English? How long before we are "found out?" How long before they recognize that we are merely a yellow shirt in disguise? How well can we hide the fact that this place is not "our home?" We are often disappointed when we are found out before we even open our mouths to say a single word. It happens more often than not.

Living in our current culture, particularly now with teenagers, this yellow shirt has often seared its image in my mind. Longings to be like everyone else, to fit in, to blend in, wow - it's overwhelming how strong the urge to strip off that yellow shirt, or cover it over with red, can be. The idea of sticking out, or shining bright yellow in a sea of red is repulsive and humbling and embarrassing. We want to lay low, to blend in. After all, sometimes it is just plain exhausting to be different.

Perhaps you can relate. Maybe you feel like you're wearing a yellow shirt and no matter how hard you try to cover it up with one that fits right in, one that doesn't stand out, one that looks just like everyone else, you can't.

Here's the thing, Scripture tells us:

Be careful so that "...you may be blameless and innocent, children of God without blemish in the midst of a crooked and twisted generation, among whom you SHINE AS LIGHTS IN THE WORLD." (Philippians 2:15).

"YOU ARE THE LIGHT OF THE WORLD. A city set on a hill CANNOT BE HIDDEN. (Matthew 5:14).

You weren't meant to wear a red shirt. You weren't designed to look just like everyone else. You, dear friend, were given a bright, shining, glorious yellow shirt, and it is the most precious gift you own. So wear your yellow shirt, my friend. Stop trying to cover it up. Stop blending in. Wear it with confidence and thankfulness that you are a LIGHT in this very dark world. Be blameless and innocent, a child of God in the midst of this broken world. Wear your yellow shirt with joy and thankfulness, and shine ever so brightly, for you are a citizen of heaven and this world is not your home.

YOUR NEW NAME

Chapter Seven

Romans 5:15-17
"But the free gift of God's undeserved grace was very different from Adam's sin…
That one sin led to punishment. But God's gift made it possible for us to be acceptable
to him, even though we have sinned many times. Death ruled like a king because
Adam had sinned. But that cannot compare with what Jesus Christ has done. God
has treated us with undeserved grace, and he has accepted us because of Jesus. And
so we will live and rule like kings."

I left work a few hours early and practically flew to my apartment - well, soon to be OUR apartment. I was leaving town to head to our wedding, and I was so excited. After throwing the last things in my bag, I loaded up my little black car and started on my way. The road out in front of my apartment was a nice, wide road with a 55 mph speed limit. At least it usually was. But that day I was passing through at a different time than normal, and, in my immense excitement, I completely forgot that I was driving through a school zone. I didn't get far before I saw the blue lights flashing behind me. I quickly pulled in to a parking lot and rolled down my window to speak to the very stern looking officer who stood before me.

I explained that I was driving through at a different time than normal, and I was so very sorry. He asked me, "What's your hurry?" I apologized profusely and said that I was actually on my way out of town to get married, I was excited, and it was a different time of day than normal. Alas, my story did not receive the sympathy I'd hoped for and I was given my first (and only) speeding ticket (to date). It was a hefty ticket, and because it was in a school zone, required driving school. It was crushing, especially as it was on the way to my wedding. What should have been an exciting trip started my wedding week with a giant, ugly bump in the road.

Fast forward, if you will, a few weeks. We were happily married and had moved my husband home to OUR apartment. One morning, I went downtown to pay my tragic ticket and handed them my brand new license with my brand new name. I told them I wanted to pay for my ticket, only there was a big problem I had not anticipated: my name had changed. They could not take my money and insisted that I go before the judge. Lucky for me, court was in session and they simply added me to the end of the docket for the day. I sat through trial after trial and patiently waited for my turn before the judge. Finally, my name was summoned and I calmly, if not awkwardly, stood before the judge.

The strong, wise looking man who sat behind the desk in front of me looked over my ticket and then asked, "How do you plead?"

"Guilty," I said.

Looking surprised, he raised his eyebrows, removed his glasses and asked, "Then why are you here?"

"I tried to pay my ticket," I said, "but because my name has changed, they said I needed to come see you."

With an interested look, he asked why my name had changed and I told him I'd just been married. "I was actually on my way to my wedding when I got the ticket," I said.

By this time, he was definitely amused, and after a few more questions, (and a jovial assertion that my officer would give a ticket to his own MOTHER), he asked to see my paperwork, so I approached the bench and handed over my marriage certificate and driver's license.

He looked it all over, handed it back and said, "Today is your lucky day. You may pay the fine, but I'm taking the points off of your license. You won't need to attend driving school, and your record will be clear."

Then, as he handed me my paperwork, he hesitated, took it back, and asked the courtroom, "Who thinks I should do better than that?" The entire courtroom erupted into cheers and applause and he smiled and said, "I've changed my mind. Your fine is forgiven. You don't owe a dime, and it's erased from your history. You can call it a wedding gift from me." As I took my documents and left the once foreboding courtroom, the remaining people stood and cheered. I walked out of that courtroom and my whole heart felt like it was smiling. I left to what felt like sunshine and rainbows, and I seriously felt like I was in a movie.

Grace. Wow, did I receive grace that day. I was guilty and I knew it. I'd committed the crime, and I'd even tried to pay for it, but something had happened: I was a bride. My name had changed. So when I stood before the judge, my new name, the fact that I belonged to my bridegroom, well…it saved me.

I deserved the penalty for my transgression that day. I was so guilty. But the judge, in his great mercy, recognized that I'd taken on the name of my bridegroom, and boy, did he offer me the most beautiful wedding gift possible: grace.

One day, my friend, we will all stand before the Great Judge, and your new name? Well, it will make all the difference.

MEMORIES WITHOUT THE SCARS

Chapter Eight

II Corinthians 5:17
"Therefore, if anyone is in Christ, the new creation has come: The old has gone, the new is here!"

Years ago, early on in our marriage, our first, precious baby was on the way. At the time we had a little black bistro-style counter height table with tall, swivel stools. Our tiny little table was really cute in our tiny little apartment, but we quickly realized that there was a major problem: there was absolutely no way we could place a high chair at this table.

After searching near and far, we found a lovely wooden table with expandable leaves that folded inside from a very reputable company on clearance. Anxious to snatch up this treasure before it disappeared, we purchased our very first "real" table for $75.00. It was the deal of a lifetime, and was our first "grown up" purchase. Our first table fit for a family.

It has served us well, these many years. All three of our children sat at this table as babies. All three have scribbled their coloring sheets here. They've sat for school projects and family conferences at this table. They've grown up before our very eyes seated at this table. We've had celebrations and we've had group struggles, laughter and tears, seated at this fine table.

Over the years, it's been covered in glitter and markers and has had deep gouges created in its top that have been irreparable. The scratches have gradually accumulated to the point that every time I look at our poor, grown up table, it drives me crazy. All I can see are the blemishes. When I gazed upon our family dinner table, all that I saw were the deep, dark scratches all over the entire top. The battle scars. The proof that this table had seen its fair share of life.

One day, I'd had enough of the battle scars, and our eldest helped me drag that table with so many memories outside where I spent the entire day sanding it down, sanding clear past the deep gouges, and making it new again.

After applying the last coat of stain, I stood back to admire my work. All the glitter is gone. The scrapes and scratches and dings have disappeared. It looks new. It's beautiful.

It made me think of the sanctifying power of our Lord. Goodness knows I am full of glitter and scrapes and dents and dings. But at some point (probably numerous times) I was dragged outside and was sanded and sanded and sanded until His very arms were sore, because He wanted me "just so." He wanted there to be millions of memories, but none of the scars. And then he took my bareness, my nakedness, and He covered me with His righteousness. Not only were the scars gone, but through His grace, I was covered, protected, stained and sealed. He wanted me to be new.

He who was seated on the throne said, "Behold, I am making everything new!" Then he said, "Write this down, for these words are trustworthy and true." Revelation 21:5

He makes all things new. He makes ME new. The process may be a lot of work. And I can't help but think that if the table could feel, the hours of sanding wouldn't just be uncomfortable...it would HURT! It would take me to my rawest, barest, most vulnerable point. But I trust in Him that He has promised to make me new, and what joy fills my soul!

Let the Great Carpenter work. Let Him make all things new. Trust Him through the hours of sanding and perseverance and sealing. Write it down, and believe He is working, for His very words are trustworthy and true. He makes ALL THINGS new...even you.

THE GREAT FEAST

Chapter Nine

Jeremiah 17:7-8
"Blessed is the man who trusts in the Lord, whose trust is in the Lord. He is like a tree planted by water, that sends out its roots by the stream, and does not fear when heat comes in, for its leaves remain green, and is not anxious in the year of drought, for it does not cease to bear fruit."

T he lazy spring days in Crete are quite predictable. You can almost most certainly bet on a perfect, cloudless blue sky. The breeze comes off of the water, cooling the earth with its luxurious, calming winds and carrying with it the deafening sounds of the cicadas.

It was on such an idyllic day that the incessant cicadean songs were interrupted abruptly. There was some intense thumping, banging and crashing coming suspiciously from the animal pen below our house. As we investigated the origin of this clattering, we found that the little sheep and goats that live just below us were hungry. They were so hungry, in fact, they were throwing their empty buckets around, just begging for help. Our hearts broke for these poor animals, and we scurried to come up with a plan. We hurried up the hill, through the gate, into our yard and began scooping up handfuls of fresh, bright green, sweet clover, mounding the dewy grasses high into empty buckets to take back to them. We stuffed our buckets full in mere minutes and traipsed our little family, buckets in hand, back to the pen to share the fresh, sweet goodness with our wooly friends.

As I walked towards the empty trough to fill it with the bounty of our abundant buckets, the little animals followed behind me. The bells around their necks were ringing jubilantly. Expectantly. They recognized what they were about to receive. Out of the blue, our son grabbed a few handfuls from the buckets and haphazardly flung them away from the skittish sheep. Immediately, every single animal stopped following me, ran away from the bountiful buckets of food, turned and violently charged the shower of green clover that had been flung to the side. There were head butts, there was moosing and nudging of the other animals out of the way. There were grunts and growls. And there was 100% concentration on the blessing that they perceived right in front of them. The bounty was forgotten and the immediate blessing was devoured. The feast was ready for them, but it was ignored, in favor of immediate, selfish pleasure.

I poured the buckets of clover into the trough so full that it was overflowing. There was so much dewy goodness. Yet I stood back and watched these animals fighting over the bits of blessing that had distracted them, all the while a huge trough dripping with three entire buckets full of abundance just sat there, waiting for them to raise their eyes and recognize the provision.

I got to thinking. Wow, I think this is a picture of me, and maybe it's a picture of you, too. Sometimes we are so starving that when our Provider enters our pen with buckets full of sweet goodness, we get excited for a moment but then manage to be consumed by the many little distractions flung our way, all the while missing the heaps of blessing that the good Lord longs to dump in front of us. He stands there, watching with compassion and understanding, and there's nothing He can do but to issue the invitation and just wait for us to raise our eyes, recognize the provision, recognize the PROVIDER, and partake in the goodness of His blessing.

Let us not be like these sheep who would be so skittish that we might be content to starve ourselves with meager blessings while great feasts sit, inviting us, awaiting our attention. Our Provider is good, and His salvation is abundant, if we would but raise our eyes away from the distractions and recognize and receive His love and care. His provision is bountiful, and it is free for the taking, if we would but open our eyes and partake.

SUNRISES, SUNSETS
AND RAINBOWS

Chapter Ten

Psalm 139:1-12
"O Lord, you have searched me and known me! You know when I sit down and when I rise up; you discern my thoughts from afar. You search out my path and my lying down and are acquainted with all my ways. Even before a word is on my tongue, behold, O Lord, you know it altogether. You hem me in, behind and before, and lay your hand upon me. Where shall I go from your Spirit? Or where shall I flee from your presence? If I ascend to heaven, you are there! If I make my bed in Sheol, you are there…'"

"**I** know you," she said with an amused smirk. "I know you're disappointed, and I know you're trying to smile despite your frustration."

"How do you know that?" I asked in amusement, for she was so perceptive, despite my best efforts to hide it. And she's only 9 years old.

"I just know you so well," she paused, then sweetly added, "If I could do something to fix it, I sure would."

To be known is a wonderful thing. To be known so intimately is a gift.

We were having one of *those* years. You know the kind. The year that seems to just keep on giving, only the things it's giving, you aren't so sure that you want. It was on one such October afternoon that I suddenly felt very unknown, as I discovered that I was a victim of identity theft. Who exactly am I, how do I prove it, who else is pretending to be me and what damage have they done? And, perhaps most importantly, how do I fix it?

I stood on our rooftop balcony (typical of the Mediterranean homes of our area) while I was on the phone, attempting to iron out all of the details of my new discovery. As I stood there, I was struck with the beauty of a rainbow in the midst of a glorious sunset with the majestic mountains behind. After the incredible sunrise we had that very morning, I felt very spoiled.

It was if God Himself had entered my very situation in those moments, and He was saying, "Even though you may feel unknown, I know you. I know you so well. And if I can create such beauty all around you to remind you of My presence, truly, I can fix this, too." And then, showing off just a little bit, He painted a rainbow in the sky and filled the atmosphere with pinks and yellows and purples.

He does know me, and He loves me, and I matter. I recognized that in the very moment of my perceived lack of identity.

Why are there such things as sunrises, sunsets and rainbows? That night, I googled it. Here's the gist:

Because the sun is so low on the horizon, sunlight has to pass through more air at sunset and sunrise than it must pass through during the day when the sun is higher in the sky. "More atmosphere means more molecules to scatter the violet and blue light away from your eyes. ... This is why sunsets are often yellow, orange, and red."

This really struck me. The beauty is there because the light is hanging so low. The beauty is there because there is more "muck" for the light to pass through, and it brings forth its radiant beauty.

Do you ever feel that life is handing you more than you can handle? Does it ever seem like if you have to pass through one more thing, you won't be able to? Does it feel as though you're just hanging so very low? It's in those moments that you find the sunrises, sunsets and rainbows. Those moments when you're at your lowest, the atmosphere swallows you up, disperses those molecules and lets beauty shine forth.

Here's to truly being known, and here's to sunrises, sunsets and rainbows.

SHELTER THROUGH THE STORM

Chapter Eleven

Psalm 91:1-2
"Whoever dwells in the shelter of the Most High will rest in the shadow of the Almighty. I will say of the LORD, 'He is my refuge and my fortress, my God, in whom I trust.'"

P ounding raindrops fell for the fourth or fifth day in a row. Winter months in Crete bring the rains, and this year was no different. The thunderstorms had been more than impressive, and we had a certain little lady sneak into our bed with us in the middle of the night several nights in a row for security, safety, and peace. It's funny - as soon as she climbs into bed with us and my arms wrap around her little frame - the sleep that eludes her is found.

Sometimes, even when thunder rumbles all around you, just knowing mom or dad is there is enough to bring rest.

This morning, Chris woke me early to tell me that our house was leaking. Sure enough, the torrential rainfall of the last few days was enough to seep inside and soak some rugs and important paperwork to its core. I set to work moving furniture, hanging rugs, draping papers all over the house to dry. I moved boxes in the garage out of the way of the impending water leaks and tried, semi-successfully, to get things under control.

Only a little while later, my phone rang. My husband's voice rang out from the other end and told me that we had yet another problem. He had gone to get gas for our little island car. He pulled up to the diesel pump (self-serve is not a thing here) and they said it wasn't working right and to pull forward to another pump. He told them twice that it took diesel and they said, "I know. Just pull up to this pump, because the normal one isn't working."

They put unleaded into our car. Our diesel car. Our car....oh, man. Our little car.

Back to being a one-car family again, I went to pick Chris up after work this evening and we realized that the trash we had put in the trunk to drive to the canister at the top of the hill had accidentally been left there all day. The stench of the car was an appropriate symbol of our entire day. It just plain stunk.

Some days, well, some days just plain stink.

On the way back up the hill to rid of our garbage, however, I was greeted with the most amazing view. Fields of olive trees, littered with grazing sheep spread out before me. The bay glittered with blues and silvers as the water swelled in the distance. Mountains jutted up into the sky, with the first dusting of the winter's snow on their peaks. And the sky shone a soft pink as the sun dipped from view. Even though lightning was flashing and thunder was rumbling in the distance, there was beauty and safety and quiet in this moment. After the storms of this week, it was as though, in the middle of the darkness, I had crept into the company of my Father, and there was safety. There was security. There was peace.

Sometimes, just knowing my Father is there is enough to bring rest. And for that, oh, I'm so thankful.

A BEAUTIFUL SONG

Chapter Twelve

Psalm 40:3
"He put a new song in my mouth, a song of praise to our God; Many will see and fear and will trust in the LORD."

From the time he was little, our eldest son has always had a basketball in his hand. I will forever picture him as that little four year old with a broken arm wrapped in a camo cast, learning in the driveway how to dribble a basketball between his legs. In my mind's eye, that will forever be my Grant. As the years have passed, his love for basketball has not changed. In fact, it could be said that he lives, eats and breathes basketball. It is his very life. As such, we spend a lot of time driving to and fro, back and forth to practice. He and I often use this time to listen to various audio books. This particular time, we had been listening to a book called, "The Inquisitor's Tale." At first I thought it was a fun, make believe story. There were sections with humorous, descriptive language picturing soldiers plunging their arms deep into piles of manure searching for something. There was even an entire chapter written on "the dragon with the fiery farts" (my mom will die if she sees I wrote that word in my book!!) But as it progresses, mixed with the levity and boyish humor is the discussion of some very profound subjects. On this particular day, the excerpt consisted of three kids trying to figure out how in the world God can be good if He allows bad things to happen.

A Minstrel happens to be there and sings them a song as an answer to their question. Initially, it seems as if this little song had absolutely nothing to do with the question at hand. In fact, it was quite a horrible song. A sad song. A tragic song. One where a man is either going to kill his son, or die himself, by the very hand of his own son. One of the kids in the book exclaimed, "That's the saddest song I've ever heard! I hated it!" But another, perhaps more introspective and perceptive one, asserts, "I love it. It's rich and beautiful and...TRUE."

The musician gently continues:

> "Life is a song, composed and sung by God. We are but characters in his song. (The man in the song) doesn't think his song is beautiful...It's not beautiful to HIM at all. But that's because he can't hear it. He's IN it. You can't hear a song you're in, right? So, if we could hear our own songs, if we could see God's creation the way God does, we would know it's the most beautiful song there is."

Let that sink in for a minute. What a beautiful picture this paints in my mind.

The kids in the story, however, continue with their angry, wounded questions: "Why would He make us suffer for a beauty we can't even see?"

While an answer is never revealed in the book, it really got me thinking. Why WOULD God make us suffer for a beauty we can't even see?

It's because OTHERS CAN! My own suffering may be so that others can marvel at the most beautiful composition written by the greatest Composer ever known. My own suffering is written into the melody of my life, so that OTHERS can see - and hear - the beauty and be drawn to Christ himself. It is creating the most beautiful melody...what a masterpiece it will one day be - whether I ever have the earthly pleasure of "hearing it" or not.

May our lives be a beautiful song, written by the greatest Composer, that others may see the beauty, and be drawn to Christ himself.

GORGE-OUS REST

Chapter Thirteen

Matthew 11:28-30
"Come to me, all you who are weary and burdened, and I will give you rest. Take my yoke upon you and learn from me, for I am gentle and humble in heart, and you will find rest for your souls. For my yoke is easy and my burden is light."

The Samaria Gorge: a deep, 10 mile long ravine with cliffs that jut into the sky on either side of you. The beauty spread out before you on this 6 or 7 hour hike is simply astounding. It takes your breath away. There's not much hiking "up" on this particular hike, but there is a lot of hiking "down." Sounds ideal, doesn't it! A beautiful hike, gorgeous scenery, walking through ancient villages and historical places and marveling at God's creation. And all of this while not having to climb upwards and get that heart rate pumping, all the huffing and puffing, the sweating...you know the feeling. The.Perfect.Hike.

It truly was...at first...

After a while, however, I felt every step. Coming down the mountain, despite recognizing God's amazing creativity and beautiful creation, well - it just plain hurt. My knees took the brunt of the descent, and it hurt. My toes were jarred in my shoes with every step, and my toenails hurt. I slid all over the rocks, and there was nothing graceful about it. It hurt. My shin connected with the jagged, pebbly rocks and when I slowly stood on my jelly legs, I had to pull the rocks out of my leg from where I had landed, and it hurt. A lot. But I could still come down the mountain. Even though I felt the pain, I could still come down the mountain. And there was so much beauty along the way, at times I barely noticed my discomfort.

One evening shortly after our adventure I was talking with a friend, processing a bit of life. Despite all of the joy, all of the amazing experiences, all of the many blessings we've encountered, life has been difficult through our transition of residing in a foreign land. In lieu of boring you with all the details of how life can go just plain wrong, how "coming down the mountain" can "just plain hurt despite the beauty all around us," I'll let you fill in the blanks, for I know your descent into the gorge has many personal stories, as well. Instead, I'll share these words that I shared with my friend:

"Today I feel like I'm standing at the bottom of a very large mountain with scraped shins and bruised toenails, looking up and knowing exactly what it is that we have to climb. We can do it. I know we can...We will get there. Slowly. And with tears. But we will get there."

Do you ever feel like you're standing at the bottom of a mountain looking up with scraped shins and bruised toenails? Here's what I realized this morning. My perspective is wrong.

The scraped shins and bruised toenails? That wasn't even the worst of it. While I continued moving down the mountain, I was ok. I could keep coming down, It hurt, but I could do it. But the next day? And the day after that? I could barely move. My muscles got tighter and tighter for a while, before I had recovered.

Sometimes the worst pain is had in the recovery. But sometimes, and this is important, God may not be asking you to climb that mountain. You may be standing there looking up in weariness, knowing what it is you have to do, psyching yourself up for the journey, but here's the kicker - He's not even asking you to climb. He's asking you to rest. He's sending you a ferry to bring you around that mountain and all the way back home. He's speaking into your very soul - "I see that mountain. And I see your bruises. And I simply want you to rest."

Do you know what a balm it is to a weary hiker to reach a place of rest? That's exactly what God is speaking to my very soul. "Quit looking at that mountain. It is not for you. Rest."

Rest, my friends. Rest in Him. God doesn't lead us to descend a deep gorge and then turn around and ascend the very same mountain right away. At least not all the time. He knows our pain, and sometimes, instead of climbing an impossible, giant mountain, he whispers into the drudgery, the pain, the bruises and the dread, "Be still, and know that I am God." Be still. Recover. And don't be in such a hurry to climb that next mountain that you forget to know, and recognize and submit to Him that "HE IS GOD." It is in that submission that healing, deep, restorative healing, can come.

So quit looking at that mountain. Just be still and KNOW that He is God. You never know - He may be sending you a ferry to bring you home, after all.

THE SHEPHERD

Chapter Fourteen

Psalm 23:1-6
    "The Lord is my shepherd; I shall not want. He makes me lie down in green pastures. He leads me beside still waters. He restores my soul. He leads me in paths of righteousness for his name's sake. Even though I walk through the valley of the shadow of death, I will fear no evil, for you are with me; your rod and your staff, they comfort me. You prepare a table before me in the presence of my enemies; you anoint my head with oil; my cup overflows. Surely goodness and mercy shall follow me all the days of my life, and I shall dwell in the house of the Lord forever."

He is a jolly older man with a beard speckled with grey and white that tumbles clear past his belly button. His face is jagged, and deep crevices form the wrinkles that can be seen around his twinkly eyes, showing the signs of lots of smiles throughout the years. He wears a baggy, green camouflage sweatshirt and blue camo pants upon his trim frame as he rides his old, beat up scooter down our old, beat up road every day, often with a cigarette hanging out of his slightly parted lips. He has a fluffy, white, friendly little sidekick that is always by his side, yapping at the wheels of his motorcycle, barking at passers by, or wrangling up the straggling sheep that inevitably lag behind.

Whenever we see him, his eyes always light up and he calls out with a, "γεια" ("Hey!"). We can't speak many other words that either one of us can understand, but we always try.

His name is Nichola. He is our shepherd.

I suspect that if you'd ask any one of us to tell you about our shepherd, our eyes would alight, a smile would come to our faces and we'd be happy to share. We all know right away who is meant when we hear the words, "our shepherd." Those two words quickly conjure up the image in each of our minds of our dear little Greek friend, Nichola.

Today I stood at our balcony and noticed a huge, concentrated flock of sheep huddled together out in the olive grove. It's not uncommon to see a concentration of sheep around here, but this was different. They were just standing there. As I watched, it became evident that one flock of sheep was standing next to our shepherd, waiting patiently, not moving an inch, while a second flock passed over the path in front of them, practically in single file. The flocks did not mix. They didn't get confused, all because of the presence of our shepherd! He got off of his bike and just stood there with them. He patiently waited for the path to clear before he gave the signal for his sheep to move.

He was a traffic light, of sorts. He stopped, so his flock stopped too. They didn't move until he did. They weren't even tempted. They were happy to stay under the leadership of their guide. It protected them. It gave them security, and it enabled them not to get lost, or even caught up with the wrong crowd, along the way.

It really got me thinking: How close are we to our Shepherd? Do we know Him intimately? Do we trust him implicitly? Do we stop when He stops so we don't get swept away by the crowd?

May we stay close to our Shepherd, this day. May we seek His leadership and security. May we stop when He stops, and only move forward when He does. May we embrace His protection, and may He so endear Himself to us (and us to Him) that we'd recognize our Shepherd anywhere. And, just perhaps, if someone asks us to share about our Shepherd, may our eyes alight and our hearts be happy to tell about Him with joy.

The Lord is our Shepherd. And oh, He is so, so good.

THE BRIDEGROOM'S RETURN

Chapter Fifteen

I Thessalonians 4:16-17
"For the Lord himself will descend from heaven with a cry of command, with the voice of an archangel, and with the sound of the trumpet of God. And the dead in Christ will rise first. Then we who are alive, who are left, will be caught up together with them in the clouds to meet the Lord in the air, and so we will always be with the Lord."

We were expectant, hopeful, and excitedly awaiting the news. We simply could not wait to hear that lockdown was ending. That's all we talked about. All we thought about. It was the first thing on our minds in the mornings and the last thing on our minds as we closed our eyes for the night. As our initial two week lockdown drew to a close, however, the first extension was announced. Then another. And another. And...well, you get the point. As predicted by those who knew more than we, full lockdown was extended by weeks. And then months. Stores were closed, activities paused. We were stuck to a 2 kilometer radius of our homes. Life had completely come to a halt. Each time the new end-date approached, I excitedly anticipated and watched for the thing I most longed for: my freedom.

Now here we were, many, many days into this thing and I'd lost track of the number of times we had been extended. It had been a lot. But one thing I noticed: at first, the extensions were depressing, tearful events. We were so deep in our anticipation that any delay was heart wrenching. As the number of extensions increased, however, the anticipation of our future freedom waned. The hope dwindled. The excitement was a distant memory. The anticipation turned to cynicism, and, if it would have happened, frankly, it would have been a surprise. We knew the day would come, but the hope was all but lost.

One morning, deep in the depths of our lockdown, I found myself thinking that my attitude was much like the attitude many of us have in the Church. We know Christ is coming again, but that anticipation seems far off, distant, even unreal in a sense. We are tired. And though we are expectant...we are only "sort of" expectant. We've stopped looking for it. If He came, frankly, it might be a surprise. My ten year old summed it up beautifully this week when she said, "I wish we could just know when Jesus is coming back. It sure would be a whole lot easier to be ready for Him and excited about the whole thing."

It sure WOULD be a lot easier to be ready if we knew. But we don't. Nonetheless, Christ wants our attitude towards his return to be like mine was at the start of this whole lockdown. As our Bridegroom, He wants to be on our minds when we rise and when we rest. He wants us to hold fast to the hope, and not allow ourselves to become jaded and tired and cynical. He wants any response to delays to bring mourning and disappointment...in the midst of holding fast to continued hope.

The reality of His return is not merely something to be hoped for. It's not solely a wish. It is something that we know will arrive. We simply don't know when. Make no mistake, it will come. Let's be ready and expectant and hopeful and waiting.

Truly, what a glorious day that will be!

INTO THE FIRE

Chapter Sixteen

T he hot, dry, Cretan summer doesn't leave much alive in its wake. What was once green and lush and inviting, is now brown and dead and crunchy - at least for the most part. There is one thing, however, that continues to grow through the drought: the olives. Through the hot summer, the olives grow faithfully on the never-ending fields of trees.

The cool, crisp days of October brings the harvest. This is when the hard work begins. It's harvest time, and the island is abuzz with the excitement of harvesting the liquid gold. Olive oil. It's nonstop labor until January or February; some part of the harvesting process is constantly in motion.

The whirring of the harvest is a constant companion for weeks on end. A long pole with several fingers on the end flick the olives from the branches and they land on a green tarp below for gathering. No sooner does the whirring end than the buzz of the chainsaws begins. The sawdust is flung high into the air, covering everything in its path with a thick layer of dust. As the buzz of the chainsaws began to fade, suddenly, we noticed as we'd look out across the backdrop of the mountainous scenery beyond our house, we saw plumes of smoke with the occasional orange tongue of fire flickering from miles away, dotting the hazy landscape. The crackle of the fire, and the musky smell it carried through the air was distinct, and comforting. At first, I thought they were burning the branches that had fallen while harvesting, but then I began noticing the trees. They had been trimmed back. Way back. To my untrained eye it looked haphazard and messy and ugly, but my husband was faithful to remind me that "they've been doing this for thousands and thousands of years. Surely they know what they're doing. Trust them."

One day, my curiosity got the best of me and I decided to research. It turns out that olive trees are trimmed back yearly for several reasons, the most important being the idea that, if good oil is desired, sunlight must penetrate each and every part of the tree every single day. If the light does not touch each fruit every day, it will not grow well and will not produce good oil. The trees are shaped yearly to allow the maximum amount of sunlight in through the branches so the maximum fruit will be produced. If the branches are too dense, olives will 1) be sparse, and 2) not produce good quality oil.

As a result, the trees are hacked and shaped with the knowledge and skill that has taken thousands of years to perfect, and then the piles of the fallen tree are lit on fire and destroyed, right there in the middle of the groves. To a casual onlooker the process can look ugly and hurtful and random and frightening (particularly when one of those unattended fires is left burning right outside of your home).

One afternoon during the middle of the harvest season, I ran across Matthew 7:17ff. "Every good tree bears good fruit, but a bad tree bears bad fruit. A good tree cannot bear bad fruit, and a bad tree cannot bear bad fruit. Every tree that does not bear good fruit is cut down and thrown into the fire..."

This fairly leapt off the page to me, as I had just studied cutting down of olive trees the day before. I'd read it before and brought my own uninformed ideas into its reading. But in this moment, I knew for perhaps the first time what Jesus meant, when he talked about good fruit and bad fruit. I knew what he meant when he said it would be cut down and thrown into the fire. I knew what his listeners pictured in their minds when he said it, and how they could conjure up the distinct smell of the burning leaves at just the remembrance of the practice.

The tree still stands. The bad fruit is removed so that the good fruit can prosper.

Be careful not to dismiss the importance of daily Sonlight, the importance of the Son touching every part of the tree every day. Learn to appreciate the constant need for pruning, both for the health of the tree, and the quality of the fruit. While it may look from the outside that Christ is just hacking away at my trunk with no rhyme or reason, and it may look ugly and strange, He knows what he's doing. And I should just...trust.

TUMBLING INTO SANCTIFICATION

Chapter Seventeen

Hebrews 12:10
"They disciplined us for a little while as they thought best; but God disciplines us for our good, in order that we may share in his holiness."

Our middle son, Mason, was given a rock tumbler for Christmas years ago. In his excitement, before he would open any more gifts, he had taken that tumbler out of the box, torn open the package of little, jagged rocks and began the process of smoothing them out into something beautiful. In my ignorance, I assumed that he would put a rough, regular rock into the tumbler, turn it on for a little while, and 20 minutes later, voila! Out would come a smooth, shiny new rock.

Magic.

But that's not how it works. First, you cover the rocks with water. And then you add the grit. Close it up tightly and put it in the tumbler for a week. But that's not all. Then you repeat the process with grit 2 for 8 days, grit 3 for 8 days and finally grit 4 for 12 days. Thirty five days total. Each grit is a little finer and less abrasive, leading to the end result: a beautiful, polished rock, free of cracks and wrinkles and blemishes. In fact, the blemishes that were once there have turned into beautiful lines of character on each rock, woven into the very core of the rock itself. They are no longer offensive, but beautiful.

Our son has cherished his rocks. He dutifully checked on them perhaps 100 times daily, interrupting their cycle, just to make sure they were doing alright, and adjusting things as needed. Between each cycle he lovingly took each rock out, rinsed it and gave it a reprieve. He examined it and admired it, and then, after a time, he lovingly placed them back into the tumbler and began again.

One day, deep into the process, he started grit 3 and he absolutely could not wait for the following 20 days to be over, for in his mind's eye, he saw what those little rocks were to become. He already envisioned the beauty that would come of them, so it was totally worth the time, concern and effort it took to get them to that point. He wanted them to be perfect and beautiful. In fact, he already saw them in his mind as the end result. So he was willing to do what it took to get them there.

So it is with us. God has taken our lives, broken rough, jagged and blemished and has thrown us into the tumbler of life . He's drowned us and added extra grit to our tumbler, sealed us up and turned it on to churn over and over again. It's not a fun process much of the time.

None of us want to suffer, but God already sees the end result. He knows what grit it will take to get us to that beautiful, shiny, polished end result, and He is willing to do what it takes to get us to that point. I know he must excitedly peek in to examine all the changes along the way at least 100 times a day, just like my Mason did.

God has taken a rough, jagged rock like me, and he's tumbling me, because He cherishes me. He already sees in His mind's eye what the end result will be, and He is so excited to get me there. The process may be long and tedious and take much longer than I think it should. But the end result is worth it.

Sanctification through suffering is like a rock tumbler. And for this, I think I am thankful for suffering. Very thankful, indeed.

CHICKEN LEG MELTDOWN

Chapter Eighteen

Matthew 19:23-24
"Then Jesus said to His disciples, 'Truly I tell you, it is hard for a rich man to enter the kingdom of heaven. Again I tell you, it is easier for a camel to pass through the eye of a needle than for a rich man to enter the kingdom of God.'"

I walked into the local butcher's shop and in broken Greek, I attempted to order chicken legs as confidently as I could. Chicken legs couldn't be so hard, right?

I walked out with chicken legs, alright. Chicken legs, still attached to chicken thighs, and worse yet, not even completely defeathered.

I'll never forget standing in my little Mediterranean kitchen and unwrapping my chicken legs from their paper that afternoon. I cried over chicken legs that day.

Sometimes, everything just seems so much harder than it needs to be. Can you relate? I'm quite sure that you can, particularly in these tumultuous times in which we are living.

The opportunity to live in another country has opened my eyes to the many, many conveniences that our home country embraces as normal, expected, every-day parts of life. Recently, someone asked me what it is that I miss the most about my home country and said I could not list the obvious - friends and family. My answer surprised me a bit: the conveniences, the ease, the intricacies of oversimplification.

Fast food. Drive-thrus. 24-hour shipping. Drone delivery. Instant everything. A million choices and variety. Online grocery shopping delivered straight to your door. Hot water whenever you want it. A physical address. Flushable toilet paper. (Yep. For real).

Get this: you can seriously buy a package of chicken legs. JUST chicken legs. A pre-packaged, 10 piece, cleanly severed package of chicken legs.

The contrast to our daily life here is profound. Most days it's fun, and exciting, and we are grateful for it. But there are those days that the differences mount and, you know, cutting up chicken legs just cues the waterworks, and cues them big time.

But as I stood in my quirky shiny red kitchen bemoaning the difficulty of severing these lifeless chicken legs and practically twisting them apart in my frustration, Jesus' life giving words were brought to mind:

"Then Jesus said to His disciples, 'Truly I tell you, it is hard for a rich man to enter the kingdom of heaven. Again I tell you, it is easier for a camel to pass through the eye of a needle than for a rich man to enter the kingdom of God.'" Matthew 19:23-24

Strange for this passage to fuel my mind as I stood crying over raw chicken. Chicken legs have nothing to do with riches...Or do they?

When Jesus says that it is hard for a rich man to enter the kingdom of Heaven, I think it is because he is pointing out a cold, hard truth: riches strip the man from the ability to NEED Christ. When we don't need Christ, we have no reason to rely on Him. And when we begin relying on ourselves, our own strength, our own money, our many conveniences, we are stripping ourselves of the opportunity to recognize our great, immense need for His grace in our every-day lives.

But here's the thing: sometimes we prefer the convenience, the riches, over the need. Of course we do. And yet, in doing so, the richness of conveniences strips us of the ability to recognize our own helpless estate. Thankfully, sometimes all it takes is the difficulty of separating chicken legs to strip us of those riches and help us recognize our deep need for Someone to come along side and shoulder the load.

Our conveniences, our money, our riches, are just like cold, lifeless, feather-stubbled chicken legs that can be torn apart at the joints: they're sure to cause disappointment and frustration. But the salvation of the Lord is marvelous, warm, and life-giving. It is well with my soul, because of Christ's life-giving work on my behalf, not because in my richness I could easily buy convenient precut chicken legs all for myself, but because in my weakness, He did it for me.

May we recognize our riches (conveniences) and may we lay them aside in favor of the life-giving sacrifice of Christ that will never disappoint.

BROKEN BARRIERS

Chapter Nineteen

Colossians 3:12-14
"Therefore, as God's chosen people, holy and dearly loved, clothe yourselves with compassion, kindness, humility, gentleness and patience. Bear with each other and forgive whatever grievances you may have against one another. Forgive as the Lord forgave you. And over all these virtues put on love, which binds them all together in perfect unity."

Nichola, our shepherd man, stood on the side of the dirt road, watching over his sheep. I had stepped outside of my gate and had started on my afternoon walk when I saw him. I cheerfully waved, he waved back and walked towards me. He's always happy to try to talk...I think the life of a shepherd is a fairly lonely one. He's trying to talk with us more, these days, and while I try so hard, most of the time I have no idea what he's saying. I often resign myself to smiles and waves and hurry on my way. Today, as I walked nearer, he reached his hand out and gave a warm high-five, of sorts. Funny, in these COVID days we are living in, how a touch, even from a stranger, can mean so much, and be so weird, all at the same time. We exchanged pleasantries and he spoke a lot of words, very fast. I told him I did not understand, so he began marching in place, gestured off into the distance and said, "Volta." Because of his actions, I recognized that he was asking me if I were going for a walk. "Nai," I replied. "Yes!"

"American?" He said, and I said, "Yes, I am American."

"No, no! "He asserted. "Volta, American speak!"

Oh! I chuckled at the term, "American speak."

"I am going for a walk," I slowly enunciated each word. He's always eager to teach me, but he's always just as eager to learn. As I walked on, I could hear him repeating, "I am going for a walk," over and over again.

As I walked, I pulled out my trusty translator app and practiced, "Pao volta," over and over again, and looked up "I am going home," "Pao spiti," in anticipation of crossing his path again. I wanted to be able to try to talk to him, as he always tries so hard to talk to me.

Sure enough, when I saw him again, I pointed in the direction of my walk and said, "Pao volta." Then I turned in the direction of my home and said, "Pao spiti." The man leapt off of his bike, jumped up and down, clapping his hands, his bubbly laughter ringing jubilantly through the evening air. "Nai, Nai!" he exclaimed. "Bravo!" He grabbed my face with both hands, kissed my cheeks at least six times and took great delight in my attempt to communicate with him.

I showed him my translator app and tried to translate a conversation but I think he found it more confusing than helpful. Nevertheless, I told him our family always enjoys seeing him and his sheep. He clapped me on the shoulder, said in broken "American speak" with the biggest smile, "Me too, my friend! I love you." I knew that word in Greek, so I exclaimed, "Oh! Sagapo!" And he once again clapped and kissed both cheeks with the biggest grin and jolly laugh, "Nai, sagapo, sagapo!"

I marveled, a little bit, as I made the rest of my trek to our home, that a little shepherd man from a village in Crete, and a backwards American family, with little ability to speak and no way to forge a relationship, could cultivate a friendship despite the barriers through smiles and waves and the occasional effort to speak a few, foreign words. How could two complete strangers exclaim "sagapo" in the middle of an olive grove and delight in the friendship of the other, despite never truly having a conversation or knowing anything about the other. Somehow, even though we can't communicate, and even though our experiences are worlds apart, he's decided that he loves our family, and he delights in our small victories with pure jubilance. And do you know, we've decided the very same thing about him. Why? Just because.

Wow - that's how life is supposed to be lived, don't you think? Wouldn't we be better off if we just plain old loved those from whom we are worlds apart?

I hope this world can be more like our little shepherd, Nichola. It would be a much better place, if you ask me.

THE SMELL THAT DOESN'T MEET THE EYES

Chapter Twenty

Isaiah 53:1-12
"He had no form or majesty that we should look at him, and no beauty that we should desire him. He was despised and rejected by men; a man of sorrows, and acquainted with grief; and as one from whom men hide their faces he was despised, and we esteemed him not. Surely he has borne our griefs and carried our sorrows; yet we esteemed him stricken, smitten by God, and afflicted. But he was wounded for our transgressions; he was crushed for our iniquities; upon him was the chastisement that brought us peace, and with his stripes we are healed."

There's a little watering hole on the back roads that we often take on the way to and from Chris' place of work. The drive is quite scenic: snow-capped mountains that stretch up to the sky on one side, rolling hills on the other, a glistening blue ocean in the distance. Sheep and goats often fill the entire road and you'll have park your car as they make their way around your vehicle. The little bells around their necks fill the air as they jingle merrily around your car. It's really quite perfect. Rolling hills, giant, gnarled olive trees as far as the eye can see, and a narrow one lane road that runs through it all. The little watering hole rests smack dab in the middle of this lovely drive.

It really is lovely. The water is always still, and the reflections it creates when it flirts with the daytime sky are quite astounding. The grey rocks mix with the grassy knolls, blossoming almond trees and distant hills, and it is quite inviting. Some would even say it is "breathtaking."

Breathtaking. Breath-taking. Never has there been a more appropriate word for this little oasis, for despite the serene beauty of this place, it has one fatal flaw: it just plain stinks.

Imagine the stench of a week old dirty diaper pail. Oh, my friend. It's worse.

And, boy, does it linger.

It is so bad, in fact, that we carry a can of Febreze in our car at all times, and when we come near to this lovely little watering hole, we preemptively spray a tropical breeze, just to lessen the blow. My kids are even convinced on the days that it's especially rank, that if they breathe it in, they'll be able to taste it. This, of course, is to be avoided at all costs, so we often drive by this picturesque little scene in silence as we all hold our breath, trying to avoid the aftermath of the crude smells that it emits. Breath-taking, indeed.

This morning, as I drove by with the colors of the sunrise still lingering in the sky, I stopped to take a picture of our little watering hole, and marveled once again at the dichotomy of my senses. At first glance, oh, how lovely it is. But linger a little longer, and recognize that it's actually rotten. And not just rotten, it's completely rancid.

As I reflected upon the scene stretched out before me, I was struck with the great contrast of the picture Scripture paints of Christ, and the picture of my watering hole that lay before my very eyes.

Isaiah 53:1-12 describes Jesus: "he had no form or majesty that we should look at him, and no beauty that we should desire him. He was despised and rejected by men; a man of sorrows, and acquainted with grief; and as one from whom men hide their faces he was despised, and we esteemed him not. Surely he has borne our griefs and carried our sorrows; yet we esteemed him stricken, smitten by God, and afflicted. But he was wounded for our trans-gressions; he was crushed for our iniquities; upon him was the chastisement that brought us peace, and with his stripes we are healed."

Ephesians 5:1-2 continues this idea when Paul asserts, "Therefore be imitators of God, as beloved children. And walk in love, as Christ loved us and gave himself up for us, a fragrant offering and sacrifice to God."

Christ's earthly life was not attractive by the world's standards. In fact, it was so horrible that we turned our eyes away, just so we could avoid seeing it. But His loving sacrifice was a fragrant, sweet aroma, holy and acceptable and pleasing to the Lord. The aroma of His sacrifice is where we find His beauty. And we get to be imita-tors of that!

We often, particularly in this social media driven world, paint a pristine picture of our lives for the world to see, but all too often, the stench beneath the picture is putrid. May this not be said of us!

May it be said that: though their lives were full of struggles, so much so that people were tempted to just "look away," they pointed to Jesus.

May it be said that: though they were ridiculed and bullied, they pointed to Jesus.

May it be said that: when trials were at their doorstep, they pointed to Jesus.

May it be said that: though their children were not perfect, they pointed to Jesus.

May it be said that: though their lives were acquainted with grief, they pointed to Jesus.

We have the opportunity this week, this very day, even, to recognize that the beauty we can see with our earthly eyes is deceptive. Our lives may not be picture perfect. In fact, they're probably not. But it's not the tidy, perfect picture that saves. It is Christ's great sacrifice on our behalf that is the sweet smelling aroma that brings salvation. We can share in that aroma, as we share in Christ's sacrifice for us.

May it not be the perfection of the appearance of our lives that others notice. May our lives be the AROMA, not the STENCH, and may it draw others into the most beautiful relationship with Christ, because of His most glorious sacrifice.

IN NEED OF OUR SHEPHERD

Chapter Twenty-One

John 10:4-14
"The gatekeeper opens the gate for him, and the sheep listen to his voice. He calls his own sheep by name and leads them out. When he has brought out all his own, he goes on ahead of them, and his sheep follow him because they know his voice. But they will never follow a stranger; in fact, they will run away from him because they do not recognize a stranger's voice...Very truly I tell you, I am the gate for the sheep. All who have come before me are thieves and robbers, but the sheep have not listened to them. I am the gate; whoever enters through me will be saved. They will come in and go out, and find pasture. The thief comes only to steal and kill and destroy; I have come that they may have life, and have it to the full."

Driving up my rocky, windy road, quite unexpectedly and from out of nowhere, a tiny baby sheep jumped right in front of my car. I swerved, it weaved, but seconds later, here it came again, straight at the danger, completely oblivious to the damage that my machine could cause to its tiny body. It was frightened. Somehow it had gotten out of its little pen and had been separated from its mother. It was crying out, dashing to and fro, and you could just see the fear in its eyes.

My eldest son was with me and he wanted to get out and try to get it to safety. He calmly and quietly approached the little lamb, but a lamb is a creature of prey, and it's only defense is to run. And run, it did.

My boy, well intentioned as he was, took off after it, scaring it more and more. It turned out that the more he tried to help, the further the sheep got from safety and the worse the situation became. This escapade continued (with lots of laughter from this momma at the sight of this little lamb dodging all of my son's efforts at help) until my Grant hopped back in the car and said, "You know what that sheep needs? He just needs his shepherd!"

Have you ever seen sheep with their shepherd? I watched it in amazement the other day as I opened my door to go for a walk. A flock of sheep was grazing outside of our gate and as soon as I opened my gate, despite my well intentioned nature, the sheep took off. There was a stampede. They were out of there. But when they reached their shepherd, they crammed all around him and he was able to walk amongst them, his fingers outstretched as he passed through their midst, lovingly touching each sheep as he passed by. They relished his presence. They wriggled, vying to get closer, delighted at his presence and his touch. They knew with him, they were safe.

It hit me like a ton of bricks the moment that my son clambered back into my car after trying his best to help: here we are, like little sheep out and about in a dangerous, truth-less, confusing world, lost and afraid. Who knows what to believe? Who knows how to respond? Oh, there are theories. And gobs of them. But where is safety? Where is truth?

Oh, yes. We are like a little lost lamb, darting around on a rocky road. There are so many people happy to help. There are so many voices happy to scream their opinions into any ear that will listen. There are so many desires to point us into what they believe is the "right direction." And these sometimes shame-inducing, well-intentioned voices are determined to help point to the "right" direction, particularly if they know your opinion is different from their own.

But do you know what occurred to me today? Oftentimes, we don't need the "help." In fact, sometimes, it only makes things worse.

You know what this world needs?

Oh, my friend. We just need the Shepherd.

NOMADIC WANDERINGS

Chapter Twenty-Two

Exodus 13:21
"By day the LORD went ahead of them in a pillar of cloud to guide them on their way and by night in a pillar of fire to give them light, so that they could travel by day or by night."

T he Promised Land. It seems we are all looking for the Promised Land these days. We are always looking for the next thing, longing for what we used to have, or looking for something better. We are quite discontent to live the lives set before us, and so we wander around, envying what others have or do, comparing our unfortunate situations, and looking for something, anything, to fulfill.

The Israelites were on the move. They'd been freed from their life of slavery and led into the wilderness. They'd been led out of a land of perceived plenty (albeit slavery) and straight into a dry, barren desert. Their desert wandering lasted 40 years. Forty.Stinking.Long.Years.

They did not know where they were going, but they knew enough to trust and to follow.

Through their wandering, they followed the cloud of God which hovered over the Ark of the Covenant. They knew that they were being guided to the Promised Land...and yet, they were stuck in the desert. They knew that in order to get there, they must follow the cloud of God. When the cloud moved, they moved. When the cloud stopped, so did they. Sometimes the cloud would pause for a few hours, sometimes days, sometimes a year or more. And yet every morning, and all day long, the Israelites would look to see if they needed to pack up their entire lives to follow God to the next place. It necessitated never really getting settled, never really feeling like they could relax, never really feeling like they were "home." Never really knowing "what's next." It required faith. It required trust. It required complete reliance upon God.

It made me think of this nomadic life that my own family is living, and now, more specifically, this life that the entire WORLD is living. Stop when the Lord stops. Only move when He moves. Watch Him. Trust Him. Seek Him. FIND Him.

What a beautiful reminder to me that it's not the world events, or my employer, or ME, that's really in charge. His instructions are simple: follow the Lord. Sometimes He stops for brief moments. Sometimes He stops much longer than I want to. Sometimes, not long enough. And yet, it is He who is in control.

So in your days of longing to settle in, longing to put down some roots, longing to move along to the "next thing," feeling too "old" to do this and dreaming of the future, longing to get back to "normal," seeking things to keep you occupied, or busy, or happy, or fulfilled, or simply just not so lonely, follow Him! Know that you are not alone. Remember that His people, thousands of years before you, knew this feeling perhaps even better than we do. He is leading. He is good. His timing is perfect, and He will get you through it! And maybe, just maybe, He is leading you to the Promised Land

PIZZA OVEN INFERNO

Chapter Twenty-Three

Daniel 3:16-18
"Shadrach, Meshach and Abednego replied to him, 'King Nebuchadnezzar, we do not need to defend ourselves before you in this matter. If we are thrown into the blazing furnace, the God we serve is able to deliver us from it, and he will deliver us from Your Majesty's hand. But even if he does not, we want you to know, Your Majesty, that we will not serve your gods or worship the image of gold you have set up."

I stood beside our wood fired oven, raging with a voracious fire, and I was seriously overwhelmed with its power. It was hot. Not just any hot; it could have been deadly.

While waiting to rotate the pizza, I could not will myself hard enough to stay there. I had to back away. I had to retreat. It was so hot that a piece of cardboard, placed in the oven several inches away from the raging flames, burst into combustion mere seconds after being placed nearby. My jeans were burning, despite the distance between myself and the outside of the oven. I had special protective gloves on my hands, a thick cotton protection over my arm, and I still could not stay for long. It was an inferno.

Shadrach, Meshach and Abednego were no strangers to this kind of fiery furnace, only on a much grander scale. When they were instructed to worship King Nebuchadnezzar's gods and bow down before his golden statue, they refused.

"Shadrach, Meshach and Abednego replied to him, 'King Nebuchadnezzar, we do not need to defend ourselves before you in this matter. If we are thrown into the blazing furnace, the God we serve is able to deliver us from it, and he will deliver us from Your Majesty's hand. But even if he does not, we want you to know, Your Majesty, that we will not serve your gods or worship the image of gold you have set up."

The Bible says that Nebuchadnezzar was so incensed that he instructed the furnace to be heated to 7 times hotter than normal. The king's strongest soldiers were wrapped up in protective clothing and instructed to lead the three to their fate. Before they could accomplish their task, however, these soldiers died because of the radiation of the heat from so far back. They were not even in the fire, they had protection, and they perished from the intensity of the heat, just from being placed nearby.

Shadrach, Meshach and Abednego plunged into the fire. I can certainly imagine the intensity. Hair-singeing, suffocating heat. Skin blistering heat. Scorching, torturous, horrible, crackling heat. Death was inevitable. It was certain. It was intended.

Imagine the shock of the onlookers when they realized that these three men, and one other, could be seen walking around in the fire. They were not burned and blistered. They were not dead. They were alive and well. Protected. Untouched.

Funny that it took a wood fired pizza oven to help me appreciate this story even more. Their faith was unwavering even in the midst of the heat. Listen to their words again, "King Nebuchadnezzar, we do not need to defend ourselves before you in this matter....the God we serve is able to deliver us...but even if he does not, we want you to know...that we will not serve your gods or worship the image of gold you have set up."

"We do not need to defend ourselves before you in this matter." How often, when faced with the heat, do we feel the need to defend ourselves? How often do we feel we have to have a reason more than, "it is God's word," especially if we are being questioned by a "king" or perhaps, in our day, an entire culture? How often when the heat is looming, do we let our tongues loose, and add to Scripture our own reasons and thoughts? The example of these three faithful men shows that we do not need to add any more words. Truth can speak for itself. Our responsibility is to stand by that truth firmly, and let truth speak for itself. We do not need to defend ourselves. God is faithful to do that for us.

Stand strong in the face of the fire. God is able to deliver you. But even if he doesn't, His truth is worth standing for.

WHO YOU ARE AND
WHOSE YOU ARE

Chapter Twenty-Four

Titus 2:6-10
"...be self-controlled. In everything be a pattern of holiness. In your teaching show integrity, seriousness, and soundness of speech that cannot be condemned, so that those who oppose you may be ashamed because they have nothing bad to say about us...so that in every way, they will make the teaching about God our Savior attractive."

We have a little saying in our house. Whenever the kids walk out the door to go to school, or visit with a friend, or anything, really, some of the last words out of my mouth as I give them a hug and send them on their way are: "Remember who you are, and Whose you are." They always roll their eyes and smile and repeat those words right along with me. While I know they know the words, the truth bears repeating and I pray the truth moves from their heads and saturates their hearts.

I'm living in a biblical treasure-trove. I've known it for some time, but recently have begun deeply studying the book of Titus. Did you know it was written to a man named Titus, a dear friend of Paul's, whom Paul had left behind on the island of Crete? Crete! That's where I live! It happened right here.

In chapter two of this rich book, Paul begins reminding Titus of who he is, and whose he is. In no uncertain terms Paul begins outlining for Titus a great reminder of how it is that he is supposed to be living and speaking and teaching. Everything that he does in word and in deed was to make men purer and better. He must, in all points of his life, show purity and freedom from all motives. He must be above seeking applause. He must aim at seriousness and truth. He must use gravity and seriousness in speech, even in private conversation, that cannot be condemned. He must never forget he is the chief teacher. He must never forget who he is. He must never forget whose he is.

Why?

Because the people are watching. The people who are trying to live the right way, but don't really know how, are watching. The people who are immersed in the local culture and don't know anything about God, well, they're watching. The people who are simply waiting for him to mess up so they can discredit his whole life? Yes. They are watching, too.

The way that Titus lives his life as a professing follower of Jesus is important, because he is reflecting the very God that he serves. He is living the words that he preaches. Christianity becomes attractive or unattractive, based upon the very people who are reflecting it.

Guess what! You, fellow believer, have a great responsibility. In this social media saturated world that we are living in, we know this more than ever before. The way that you live your life and the words that come out of your mouth matter! You are reflecting your Creator, and the ways that you interact with others (even in a vitriolic political season), matters. My life can either draw others closer to Jesus, or it can push them away.

So how are we to live:

> "...be self-controlled. In everything be a pattern (this means it can be copied) of holiness. In your teaching show integrity (uncorruptness), seriousness (gravity - whatever

will ensure respect in character), and soundness of speech (incapable of decay, purity) that cannot be condemned, so that those who oppose you may be ashamed because they have nothing bad to say about us...so that in every way, they will make the teaching about God our Savior attractive." Titus 2:6-10 (I added some exposition of what the original words intended in parentheses).

Friends, as you are sent out into this dark and dreary world, remember who you are, and remember Whose you are. Be holy, as He is holy (1 Peter 1:16). It matters.

THE CONCERTMASTER

Chapter Twenty-Five

Joshua 1:8
"Keep this Book of the Law always on your lips; meditate on it day and night, so that you may be careful to do everything written in it. Then you will be prosperous and successful."

◆ ◆ ◆

M usic is the pathway to my soul. My husband, knowing my affinity for the arts, surprised me one year for my birthday. Despite his very small appreciation for the classical arts, he planned a night out with a special dinner and a surprise visit to the local symphony. A date-night dream come true! It had been years since I'd been to a symphony, and as I sat there watching, I was struck as the Concert Master, prior to the start of every single piece, would stand up and tune the entire orchestra. Before they began anything, even if they were in tune moments before, they took the time to ensure they were in tune right now. This very moment mattered.

I spent the days following our concert, not replaying the music in my mind as I often do, but replaying the actions of that orchestra. There are so many beautiful implications of that discipline, but the one that stuck out the most to me that day was the idea of the importance of ensuring that I am in tune. It doesn't matter if I think I need it or not. It doesn't matter that I was in tune moments before. It doesn't even matter how many times I've done it before. Before I begin ANYthing, I need to make sure I'm in tune. How do I do that? Prayer and Scripture reading. Oh, it's so important! It truly is a discipline. It's something I must make myself do. And if I don't do it, my life can quickly fall out of harmony with the rest of the "orchestra" and produce disastrous results.

Be the Concert Master of your life. Practice those disciplines that will keep you in tune, stay plugged in to the written "music…" and don't begin anything new until you've tuned in! The results, when under the direction and tutelage of the Great Conductor, are simply masterful.

BALLISTIC PEACE

Chapter Twenty-Six

Colossians 3:16
"Let the message of Christ dwell among you richly as you teach and admonish one another with all wisdom through psalms, hymns and spiritual songs, singing to God with gratitude in your hearts."

I don't think there has ever been a time where I felt the way I did that January morning when my phone started blasting a horrible siren sound. To see a ballistic missile was headed straight toward us in Hawaii...there are simply no words to convey our feelings in that moment. We had a plan for an event such as this one, and it worked beautifully. But as I ran around the house closing all blinds, securing all doors, scooping our sleeping children out of their beds and even trying to call our loved ones to say our final farewells, I could truly hardly breathe.

As our family huddled into the little closet hidden beneath our stairs, holding our crying babies, however, the only thing that we could do, was worship. We had the sweetest time of prayer, claiming that God had not given us a spirit of fear but of power, of love, and a sound mind. We prayed for those in our state and world that do not know the Lord, we prayed for the one who had launched such a missile (which turned out to be just a massive mistake and misunderstanding), and while the tears still flowed in sadness, my breath returned and sweet peace enveloped us.

When our kids were babies, when they needed calming, we had a special song that we made up for each of them that we would sing. Every night before bed, we'd sing them each their songs. Any time they'd been hurt and needed comforting, we'd sing their songs. Any time we just wanted them to know we loved them, we'd sing them their songs. And so, as we huddled there, crammed into our tiny space together, thinking these might be our last moments on earth, we sang them their songs once again, wondering if it might be for the last time. It was to calm them, yes. But it was for me, too. To give me strength as a mom, and to help me express my love to them.

Our songs changed to songs of worship, and we all sang together, speaking words of truth even while anticipating every noise, every shake, every rumble. It was as we sang songs of worship as a family that I realized that all of these years I've sung to the Lord, I thought it was for Him. And it is...He desires our worship and praise. But in these moments of life that are harrowing and intense, these songs are for me. They keep me grounded. They keep me speaking truth. They bring me from a place of fear, to a place of trust, a place of peace. They give me strength and they help me to express my love and trust in a tangible way...even to the very end.

Immerse yourself in Scripture. Ground yourself in hymns and spiritual songs. It is for His glory. But it is for you, as well. The peace He brings is a beautiful thing.

WE DON'T RECEIVE
WHAT WE DESERVE

Chapter Twenty-Seven

Jeremiah 31: 3-5
"I have loved you with an everlasting love; I have drawn you with unfailing kindness. I will build you up again, and you will be rebuilt. Again you will take up your timbrels and go out to dance with the joyful."

Easter is Greece's most important and widely celebrated holiday. On Holy Saturday, Greece traditionally celebrates (typically at midnight) that Christ has resurrected. A flame is flown from Jerusalem to Athens, and then it is distributed to the various villages throughout the country. At the close of the service, the light (the flame from Jerusalem) is distributed to the people and it gradually spills out of the doors of the church, into the communities and villages. The symbolism to me was quite beautiful. The Light of Christ spills forth and goes into all of the world. Christ is risen! Hallelujah! (People even drive home with their candles still lit so that they can symbolically bring the light into their very homes).

And then, in an interesting, dramatic and even seemingly fun, turn of events, as the church bells jubilantly ring, and the flickering candles spread all through the villages, those holding the light of Christ immediately turn around as they jubilantly cheer loudly and send off fireworks and shotguns as they literally burn a likeness of Judah (Judas). Why? Well, after asking several people, most said they didn't know; it was just something they did each and every year. But one older gentleman, anxious to help me understand, asserted that it was "because Judas had betrayed

Jesus and he was just a 'really bad guy.'"

No sooner had the light of Christ symbolically entered the world than we holding that light, pointed the finger of condemnation to one man. One man became the villain. One man became hated. One man took the blame and held the fault of the entire glorious crucifixion, and that one man had to be punished. And yes, we delighted in it.

I stood at first in amusement, and then in horror, and then in tears, even propping myself against an ancient column in a sea of flickering candle light, for fear of collapsing in grief. The moment, seconds before, was ripe. The possibility of proclaiming the Gospel was pregnant with possibility. But instead of grasping our glorious hope, we looked at the one, and condemned him. We condemned him for betraying Jesus. We condemned him and blamed him and celebrated his horrific demise, and we forgot that we, ourselves, are him! We are the guilty ones. We are the betrayers. We are the sinful. We deserve that voracious fire, and much worse. The penalty for our sins is horrific death. And we deserve every bit of it.

Oh, but the glorious cross, my friends. The glorious, glorious cross. Because of the cross, Jesus was flung into hell, and suffered that blistering fire, on my behalf. And because of the resurrection, I never, ever have to be, even though I deserve it with every single ounce of my being. And just like He died for me, Jesus, my friends, well, he even died for Judas.

How like us to barely grasp the glorious hope offered freely to us, and then to immediately turn our backs to it, to celebrate the demise and destruction of another. How like us, to forget the weight of our own sin, and to recognize the sin of another. How like us, to believe the best in ourselves and not recognize our own sinful propensities. How like us to claim the free gift of grace for ourselves, and to deny it from another. How like us to forget, and how like us to simply get it all wrong.

Let us not grasp the Glorious Light, allowing it to spill into our streets, and then squelch it by pointing the fingers of condemnation. Oh, my friends, let us grasp that Glorious Light, humbly remember what we ourselves deserve, and spread that Light into the very ends of this earth. That, my friends, is Easter.

Christ is Risen. Hallelujah.

LOVE LETTERS

Chapter Twenty-Eight

Romans 5:8
"But God demonstrates his own love for us in this: While we were still sinners, Christ died for us."

L ove. It's a powerful thing, isn't it? A reminder that we are not given up on, we are cherished and someone thinks we are special...it can keep us going for a long time. So instead of buying them little trinkets and candies for Valentine's Day this year, I sat down and set out with the goal of writing a list of 170 things that I love about each one of our dear children. That's a lot of reasons. 510 individual reasons (and I just keep coming up with more).

I was quite certain that they'd open my letters on Valentine's morning and smile, and perhaps skim over their lists, but I never dreamed that there was any way that they would each sit there and intently read the entire six pages of single spaced reasons why I love them. To my great surprise, they did. They sat there for a very long time, sometimes with smiles on their faces, sometimes with tears in their eyes. Sometimes, they'd laugh, and occasionally they would even share one they especially liked out loud. They read, and ruminated upon, and digested every single word. And when it was all over, one sweet kid wrapped his arms around me and whispered, "Thank you for never giving up on me."

It occurred to me as we sat there snuggled up together as a family on that Sunday morning enjoying the words of love written specifically for each one of my precious children, that the words that poured forth from my heart to my children pale in comparison and are only a mere reflection of the love letter that God has written to me, to us. He wrote every word with me in mind. He longs for me to devour his Word like I longed for my kids to devour mine. He nudges me, and invites me with great hope. Sadly, instead of delighting in His great love for me, this greatest Love Letter ever written sometimes just stays on my table, unopened, and un-devoured.

What a shame it would be to allow that sweet Love Letter to sit, unopened on your coffee table. Imagine the joy your Father feels when you read and meditate upon His words of love. After all, He wrote every single word in pursuit of you. Truly, the greatest love story ever written, was written just for you. And after reading these great words of love, you can reach up to heaven, and with tears in your eyes, you can say to your Father, "Thank you for never giving up on me."

NOT HORSIN' AROUND

Chapter Twenty-Nine

"For this very reason, make every effort to supplement your faith with virtue, and virtue with knowledge, and knowledge with self-control, and self-control with steadfastness, and steadfastness with godliness, and godliness, and godliness with brotherly affection, and brotherly affection with love. For if these qualities are yours and are increasing, they keep you from being ineffective or unfruitful in the knowledge of our Lord Jesus Christ. For whoever lacks these qualities is so nearsighted that he is blind, having forgotten that he was cleansed from his former sins..."

She spent months perfecting her trot. We'd driven up the windy roads into the mountains once a week where our daughter would hop on a horse and work on improving her horse riding skills an hour and a half at a time for months now. At first, it was exciting every week. She'd looked forward to going all week long. But before long, her challenges became less and less, and she found that riding around in circles, connected to a rope and not really doing anything on her own, was just plain stifling. She was tired of trotting and dreamed of bigger challenges, but there was one problem: the horses themselves. They were "beginner-rider" kind of horses. They were great on the lead, but if you asked them to do anything more advanced, they refused.

Recently, another horseback riding option became available and we switched programs. The very first week was like a night and day difference. It was a breath of fresh air. Where before if she weren't on the lead, her horse would stubbornly plant his hooves in the sand and refuse to move, this time her horse practically sacheted across the arena, allowing her to work with him in tandem. He responded to her every request and he was happy to leap, prance, gallop and jump all around that arena. That girl was flying around, her hair spread wide in the wind behind her with a jubilant laugh rippling from her smiling lips. She was having the time of her life.

So it is with our Christian life, my friend. When we start out, we need to be on the lead. We need the help of a mentor to keep us going and teach us the basics. After a while, a walk becomes a trot, and if you're lucky, every now and then you might even get to run. But before long, and naturally so, we long for more.

Riding around in circles while being connected to a rope was not what we were made for in our Christian journey. One day, you make the leap, and it's not until you're out there in that arena all on your own, trusting in the truths you've learned all along through Scripture, study, prayer and mentorship, that you find out that you can fly. Suddenly, all those hours spent training have given you wings, and you'll find yourself sacheting and having the time of your life.

Stick with the basics. Plug in to Scripture. Spend time in prayer. But cut the rope, my friend. Start with a trot, but don't stay there. Get out there, get the wind in your hair, and fly.

THE WORLD IS ON FIRE

Chapter Thirty

Deuteronomy 13:4
"You shall follow the Lord your God and fear him; and you shall keep his commandments, listen to His voice, serve Him and cling to Him."

R ecent world events were the topic of our lengthy phone conversation. As we said our goodbyes, she exaggeratingly and humorously said "So the world is on fire...have a great day." Wow. This really hit home and got me thinking.

As we were preparing to move our entire household this most recent time, because of many things out of our control, our life was turned upside down. There were so many days where I felt defeated, tired, overwhelmed and unsure of what the future may look like. There was some fear. There was some peace. There were days of mourning and there were days of hope. Our plans were made on a day by day basis. Emotions ran high. Patience ran low. Our own little personal world was on fire. Sometimes it was smoldering. Sometimes it was in raging flames.

Each of the five members of our family processed things a bit differently than the others, and we ended up wounding each other because of our lack of understanding and our inability to put ourselves outside of self to see things from another perspective. Self was important. Everyone else...well, they weren't so much. We were all surviving, and even though we loved each other, self preservation became a main goal for all involved.

As we trudged through these days, TRUTH became my lifeline. If I weren't drowning myself in truth, I was drowning in deceit. I made a playlist to play over and over again, I intentionally sang words of truth and peace, and I prayed the words over my family. What a difference it made in my own perspective.

In recent years, our world has really taken - and given - a beating. We've wounded each other through words and actions and we've grieved ourselves both in recent days as well as in the many long days of our past. Self preservation runs high on all sides of issues. Everyone else...well, they just seem to not matter. I get it! We are in survival mode! Self preservation is our natural inclination.

The Lord knows our pain. He is already aware of the hurts, but He desires to hear your lips call out to Him.

Speak words of life over your community, country and world. Marinate your mind and bathe your heart in words of Truth. Make sure your life is in line with Scripture, and hold fast to things that are holy.

Change does need to happen. But TRUTH needs to be our lifeline. If our change is not cloaked in truth, it is a change not worth having.

So...the world is on fire. Let us cling to the Living Water and not fan the flames, or worse, burn down with it.

Made in the USA
Las Vegas, NV
11 November 2021